RADSTOCK &
MIDSOMER NORTON
THROUGH TIME
Lorna Boyd

AMBERLEY PUBLISHING

Ludlow Farm, Radstock
A view across Ludlow Farm to Radstock, taken from the Frome Road turnpike in 1871. The large building centre left is the Waldegrave Arms, with the Middle Pit chimney visible just behind.

For George, with thanks for your patience and encouragement;
and for our grandchildren Isaac, Evelyn, Lucy, Isobel and Genevieve.

First published 2013

Amberley Publishing
The Hill, Stroud, Gloucestershire, GL5 4EP
www.amberley-books.com

Copyright © Lorna Boyd, 2013

The right of Lorna Boyd to be identified as the
Author of this work has been asserted in accordance with
the Copyrights, Designs and Patents Act 1988.

ISBN 978 1 4456 1527 1 (print)
ISBN 978 1 4456 1550 9 (ebook)

British Library Cataloguing in Publication Data.
A catalogue record for this book is available from the
British Library.

Typesetting by Amberley Publishing.
Printed in Great Britain.

Introduction

Roald Dahl, before he became famous, wrote in his autobiography about his employment in the 1930s:

> My kerosene motor-tanker had a tap at the back and when I rolled into Shepton Mallett or Midsomer Norton or Peasedown St John or Huish Champflower, the old girls and the young maidens would hear the roar of my motor and would come out of their cottages with jugs and buckets to buy a gallon of kerosene for their lamps and their heaters ... Nobody gets a nervous breakdown or a heart attack from selling kerosene to gentle country folk from the back of a tanker in Somerset on a fine summer's day.

The two ancient settlements of Radstock and Midsomer Norton are situated in the centre of the North East Somerset coalfields. There are several Bronze Age and Iron Age features in the surrounding area and there is also good evidence of Romano-British activity, with the Roman Fosse Way passing close by. Both towns and their environs are designated conservation areas, and several attractive walking, riding and cycling tracks traverse the area, some passing by the sites of a number of the scenes and buildings included in this book.

Radstock was mentioned in Domesday as 'Stoche', from the Old English for a stockade. The 'rad' part of the name may be derived from the local reddish-coloured soil, though another suggestion is that it is a corruption of 'rood', referring to a preaching cross set up before the church was built.

It remained a small village until coal mining became important here in the eighteenth century, after which it quickly grew to become the centre of the North East Somerset coalfields. Complex geology and narrow seams made coal working extremely difficult, but it provided welcome employment for the local men and boys; women and girls were never employed in Somerset coal mines. With the coming of a coal canal, tramways and the railways, the population increased and many homes, usually in terraces, were built on the surrounding hillsides. With its last pit closing in 1973, it is now recognised as one of the best preserved former mining towns in the country.

Though it is disputed whether Midsomer Norton is the 'Nortone' mentioned in the Exon Domesday, there was clearly an early thriving settlement in the area. The first definite documentary evidence dates from 1180, when it was recorded that Merton Priory, Surrey, owned a manor here. 'Norton' means 'a place north of somewhere else'. The 'Midsomer' part of the name is possibly derived from the Midsummer festival that is linked to St John the Baptist, patron saint of the local parish church; though it could just denote its location on the River Somer. It was certainly known as Midsomer Norton by 1248, as it is mentioned in a Royal Charter of that date, when Henry III granted Huge de Vivonia the important right to hold an annual three-day fair at his manor there. This appears to have been a cattle fair originally and was held in The Island and down through the High Street. By the late nineteenth century it had become a one-day event and a funfair added to its attractions. Although discontinued in the 1970s, the fair was recently resurrected as an annual event once more.

Coal mining and the coming of the railway were also important developments in Midsomer Norton's history. The town's railway station was immortalised in the 1963 Flanders and Swann lyrics for 'Slow Train', lamenting the Beeching closures:

No more will I go to Blandford Forum and Mortehoe
On the slow train from Midsomer Norton and Munby Road
No churns, no porter, no cat on a seat
At Chorlton-cum-Hardy or Chester-le-Street
We won't be meeting you
On the slow train...

Both towns also had important brewing, bootmaking and printing factories, to name but a few, as well as industries associated with mining and the railways. The noise and dirt must have been all-pervasive at times, but with an accompanying sense of bustle and liveliness!

It is so important that the rich heritage of these two towns and their environs continues to be preserved and celebrated and, as the granddaughter of several generations of local coal miners, I hope that this book plays a small part in that process. I feel privileged to have met so many people who have been willing to help me and to share their knowledge of the area and its history, while appreciating the need for sensitive change and development.

Lorna Boyd
2013

View Across Radstock

The domination of the railway tracks through the centre of the town can clearly be seen in this early twentieth-century view. Note the Methodist church in the centre and Wells Hill running up from the mid-right-hand side. The surrounding fields show that the area had a combination of both rural and industrial usage. Because of the extensive tree planting and building of recent years, taking views like the one above is now very difficult; the image below was taken from the opposite side of the valley.

St Nicholas's Church, Radstock

It is probable that a Norman church existed here, though the oldest parts still existing, the porch, tower and part of the south wall, are dated to the late fourteenth century. The church was extensively rebuilt in 1879. There is an alabaster pulpit, erected by public conscription in 1899, in memory of the grandson of Admiral Lord Nelson, the Revd Horatio Ward, BA, Rector of the Parish from 1853–88. There is also a Norman font, rescued from a neighbouring farmyard where it had long been used as a cattle trough.

St Nicholas's Church, Radstock

On the right of the porch entrance is a fourteenth-century primitive scratch dial, which was designed to mark the hour of the Mass. There is also sundial on the south wall, designed by Clementine Bax in 1924, with an inscription beneath it:

When as a child I laughed and wept, Time crept, When as a youth I thought and talked, Time walked, When I became a full grown man, Time ran, When older still I daily grew, Time flew, Soon I shall find in passing on, Time gone. Whence? Why? Whither?

Bathing Pool, Radstock

Postmarked 1907, this postcard shows Waterside stream. It was dammed here at the delightfully named 'Snail's Brook' so that a pool could collect for bathing. It was well used, especially by miners and local children. The changing rooms have, unfortunately, disappeared, but there are plans to restore the site for use as a wild swimming site. The large building on the hill above was South Hill House, since demolished.

The Bridge, Radstock, 1805

This picture, used by kind permission of the artist David Fisher, depicts Radstock and the Somerset Coal Canal as they would have looked in 1805. Here, seen running alongside the present Waterloo Road, coal was transported from Radstock to the Midford Locks from the late 1790s to around 1815. The canal was replaced by a tramway until this, too, was superseded by the railways. The arch of the bridge over the River Somer can just be seen on the left, just below the wagon. The building on the right is now the Radstock Hotel. William Smith's work on surveying for the canal led him to identifying predictable patterns in strata and fossil remains, resulting in him becoming known as the 'Father of English Geology'. The Memorial Garden, seen in the picture below, was built on the site of the canal and railway and opened in 2005. The pit wheel was formerly used at Kilmersdon Colliery, one of the last pits to be closed in the area in 1973.

Church Street, Radstock

This scene, looking towards the St Nicholas's church, has not changed a great deal, except you have to take great care crossing the road here now! The Victoria Hall on the left and the large house on the right are recognisable by their architectural features, but the beautiful lamp has sadly gone. The children may have been on their way to the school near the church in the background, although judging by their clothes they were probably attending Sunday school.

The Street, Radstock

This was probably taken about 1900, as the signal box, which can be seen in the background on the left, was rebuilt in 1909. The view is from Wells Hill towards The Street and again shows little change in the buildings and general road layout. The Wilts & Dorset Bank is on the right. Adjoining this, just out of sight in the picture above, was Purnell's printing and stationery shop. In the early 1800s, a George Bince lived in a cottage on that site, from where he would distribute the poor relief fund.

The Street, Radstock

This view, probably dating from the 1950s, shows some shops, the back of the Methodist church and a row of cottages. This scene has changed little, except for the addition of many parked cars and the losses of the church's small spire, due to unsafe beams, and the cottages' boundary walls. The cottages have since been converted to form Hope House Surgery.

Radstock House, The Street

This late eighteenth-century building, possibly incorporating an older structure, was previously called Radstock Manor House and was home to Squire John Smith. In 1855 it was auctioned and bought as a family home by George Coombs, who lived there until his death in 1908. He was the first chairman and managing director of Messrs Coombs, Clandown & Radstock Breweries and Hotels Co. Ltd. It is now the Radstock Working Men's Club. In 1870, he sold one of his orchards to the Great Western Railway to build a stationmaster's house and when this was demolished the present library was built.

The Street Towards Bath Road, Radstock
Of note in this image dating from the early 1900s is that the two ivy-covered buildings have been cleared and had bay extensions added; however, the lines of the small boundary walls have remained intact. Note the distinctive three-storey, arched-windowed façade of Clement's Drug Store on the right, now Automania, though the doorway has been converted to a window.

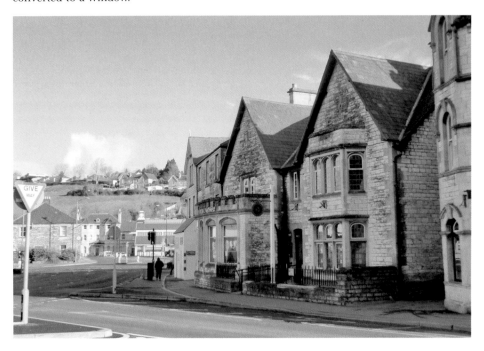

Wells Hill, Radstock

From the early 1900s, apart from the loss of the building on the right, where the two women are walking, this view of Wells Hill is instantly recognisable. The building with the distinctive arched windows and doorways held the original Co-operative shop. Mr Steggle's photography shop was on the opposite side of the road to where the horse and cart is standing, with George West's cycle shop next to that. The Radstock Co-operative Society started trading in 1868 and the store in its present form, on the opposite side of the road with all departments under one roof, opened in 1979.

Baptist Church, Wells Hill, Radstock
This early twentieth-century view belongs to a gentleman who was married here during the Second World War. The steps, as can be seen, originally came right down to the road, but it is thought that they were demolished by a runaway lorry in the 1930s. The chapel was built in 1842 and is still used for worship today. Note the adjoining shop with its adverting boards. This is now a private dwelling with its door – sensibly, given current traffic conditions – having been moved round to the side. Otherwise, little has changed in the exteriors of both buildings.

Towards Wells Hill, Radstock

This 1895 view clearly shows the Great Western Railway set of level-crossing gates with the station fencing and a train signal on the left. The building with the arched doorway was Parsons, a grocer, draper and wine merchant's that is a now hairdressing salon.

From The Bridge Towards Wells Hill, Radstock

The Bristol Artillery leaving the centre of Radstock, heading towards Bath, following a recruitment visit; it was taken from an identical position to the previous page, but dates to the First World War. The modern view shows the Co-operative supermarket that stands on the site of the former rectory, hidden by the hedge in the photograph above. In the rectory grounds there was also a stone-built bathing house, where the rector would often take a cold spring-water bath. This was all demolished and replaced by the new Radstock Co-operative Society supermarket in 1979, an independent store that reduced prices during the miners' strikes of the early twentieth century to try to help local families.

Fortescue Road, Radstock

This view, looking towards the centre of Radstock, probably dates to the 1950s and shows a general house furnisher store in the left foreground. This row of shops was built in the 1890s, some retaining original roller shutters on their windows, suggesting some unruly behaviour in former times! Although some renovations have been made, they still differ greatly from the typical 1960s-built shops, seen below, that replaced those on the right-hand side of the road.

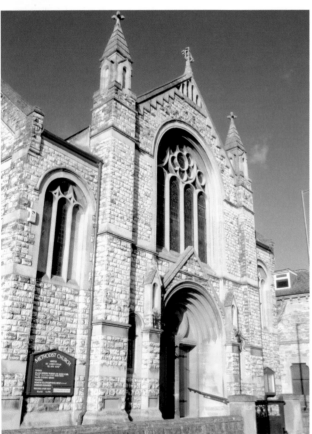

Methodist Church, Fortescue Road

This church, with its adjoining schoolroom, was opened in 1902, when the congregation moved here from its former chapel in Coombend. The opening, despite heavy rain, was attended by large crowds and was a great celebration. The festivities were presided over by Alderman James McMurtrie of South Hill House, the manager of the Countess of Waldegrave's collieries.

Great Western Railway, Radstock

This steam train would have started out from Bristol and run south-easterly through Radstock to Frome, where it joined the line from London Paddington to Plymouth and Penzance. The station opened on 3 September 1873. It was situated just beyond Frome Road and a small subway allowed passengers to walk from Victoria Square, under the rail tracks, on to Frome Road, opposite the present Charlton Timber Company premises. The original signal box was operational from 1874 and was rebuilt in 1909, the above photograph dating to about 1905. The station closed to passengers in 1959, the station buildings were demolished in 1963 and eventually the railway closed for all traffic in 1965. The Waldegrave Arms and the Big Pit chimney can be seen in the background. The signal box was taken to Didcot Railway Centre in 1975, where it was completely renovated and is on display. The site is now awaiting regeneration.

Somerset & Dorset Railway, Radstock

Note the Market Hall clock tower in the centre background of this image, taken in 1904. It is still to be seen today. This line started at Bath, taking a westerly course through Radstock, finally terminating at Templecombe Junction, which was on the main line of the Southern Railway running between London and north Cornwall. This station was opened on 20 July 1874. The station had two platforms that were connected by a footbridge and was situated in Waterloo Road, just along from the Market Hall on the opposite side of the road. The station closed to passengers in 1966 and for coal in 1973. The image below was taken from the position of the original station site, now a car park, and the buildings that still exist can be seen quite clearly.

Somerset & Dorset Railway, Radstock

Taken in 1963, this picture shows clearly the footbridge, the platforms, and Waterloo Road with its cottages on the right. Having two railways running through the town caused problems from the start. Within weeks of opening, the two parallel level crossings were generating complaints and Colonel Yolland was despatched by the Board of Trade to investigate: he concluded that they were dangerous and objectionable and that there should be regulations preventing such a situation happening in the future. Records from 1902 show that around fifty trains a day ran along this line on a typical Saturday alone. In the view below, looking towards the direction the train is taking, standing next to the river is a large building, which was erected in 1915 as the Radstock Co-operative Bakery. The flour was mostly brought in by train and loaded on to a raised platform, where the present car park is, then hoisted up to the upper floors.

Towards the Market Hall, Radstock

The Co-operative store now dominates the left-hand side of the road at this point. The level-crossing gates and signal box have disappeared, but otherwise the architecture is relatively unchanged. The car in the foreground, with its boot facing us, was a Standard Vanguard and belonged to Dr Gibb Thompson.

Bath Road, Radstock

Taken in 1974, this photograph shows the moving of a 1930s Sentinel S4 platform truck, owned by John and Vince Goold of Camerton. On the left is the Radstock Hotel, built in the mid-nineteenth century on the site of an older building. It was originally called the Waldegrave Arms, named for the Waldegrave family who had been the Lords of the Manor of Radstock since the Civil War and who became the owners of many of the local collieries. Radstock's first horse-drawn fire engine was kept at the back of the inn in the 1890s.

The Bridge, Radstock
Built in 1909, the Chivers family ran a large hairdresser's and tobacconist's shop in the right-hand side of this large building. It is now home to a popular bicycle shop that attracts customers from far and wide. There are remarkably few architectural differences to be seen between the two pictures.

Casswell, The Bridge, Radstock

This ironmonger's shop was built in the early twentieth century. Its stock included mining carbide lamps and refills, and also the tin baths used for bathing in front of the kitchen ranges. There have been some renovations since the 1930s, when the above photograph was taken, but it is still recognisably the same building today, though divided to provide a music shop and a hairdresser's.

The Bridge, Radstock

This postcard probably dates to the 1930s and is particularly interesting for the clear view it shows of the Somerset & Dorset Railway level-crossing gates on the right. The gentleman is looking at the window display of Casswell's hardware and ironmongery shop.

Sparey's Newsagent, Radstock

On the corner of Frome Road, Mr Sparey is selling newspapers outside his small shop in the 1930s. He was originally a miner, but following the 1926 General Strike he decided he wanted to start his own small business. The railway signal box and the Market Hall are both evident in the background. The shop building, seen below, is currently unused and is awaiting sale or rental.

Market Square, Radstock

A view of some of the outside stalls on a busy market day in the early twentieth century. The Bell, with its adjoining buildings, was a large brewery business and provided alternative employment to the local mines. Seen below, The Bell was converted to provide nine community flats in 2003.

The Bell, Radstock

This photograph dates to around 1900. Before the railways arrived, the mail coach delivered letters to The Bell, where they were sorted and delivered to the surrounding district. It was an old building that was rebuilt by its owner, George Coombs, in 1880. Mr Coombs, the gentlemen in the centre wearing the light-coloured overcoat, was a major brewer in the area and founded the Radstock fire brigade. The market yard, a little further along Waterloo Road, was also used for a weekly cattle market and for events such as travelling fairs and prizefights.

Radstock Market, Radstock

Taken around 1900, this image shows Waterloo Road as little more than a lane at this time. Just visible beyond the market to the right is a small row of cottages. A Dame School was held in one of these in the early nineteenth century, and a little further along were terraces of cottages built for workers and their families in the late 1800s by Lady Waldegrave. In 1989, a collection was started by volunteers determined to preserve the mining heritage of the area, in a barn in Haydon. With the help of Lottery funding it moved to the Market Hall building, opening in 1999 and developing into a highly regarded museum.

Radstock Market, Interior

A market was held on Saturdays, with local traders selling meat, vegetables and general produce. Until 1897, when the present hall was built by local brewers Messrs Coombs at a cost of £2,500, it had originally consisted of a number of open-fronted sheds surrounded by a low boundary wall and railings. It now houses the museum's collection and provides a venue for exhibitions and a range of educational and social events.

Victoria Square, Radstock

Photographed in the early 1920s, formerly called the Working Mens' Institute, the Victoria Hall was erected in 1866 with the help of Lady Waldegrave. In 1897, it was enlarged, renovated and renamed to commemorate Queen Victoria's Diamond Jubilee. Originally it held a library, a reading room, recreation and billiards rooms, and a hall for meetings, public entertainments and the Petty Sessions Court. On the opposite side of the square was Fortescue House, now incorporated into the post office sorting centre. This was originally a college, opened in 1882 for young gentlemen, and later also for young women, for vocational education. To the left of the original cenotaph site, just behind the parked vehicle, is a small underpass that is still in use today and allows pedestrians to walk under the railway tracks to Frome Road.

The Cenotaph, Radstock

This image shows the ceremonial unveiling of the war memorial in Victoria Square in around 1922. Note the steam train running behind the cenotaph and the people standing on top of the rail track underpass just behind the flag. The cenotaph stayed in Victoria Square until it was moved to its present position, the Memorial Garden in Waterloo Road, in 2005. The cream-coloured plaque below shows its original position.

The Radstock Co-operative Delivery Van

Almost certainly photographed during the First World War, this horse-drawn delivery van was well-known and appreciated in the area for many years for delivering bread and cakes. The renovated van is shown on a rare outing below, with the important task of delivering Father Christmas to his grotto in the Co-operative store. The van can now be seen as an exhibit in Radstock Museum.

Whitelands Terraces, Radstock

These were the first purpose-built miner's terraces in Radstock built in the 1840s, though only the two lower of the original four terraces remain. They are unusual because they have three storeys instead of the usual two, and because the terraces are much longer than was usual. The toilets, or 'privies', were at the back of the terraces, and the long front gardens ensured that many vegetables could be grown and also allowed families to keep a pig.

The Mill, Radstock

Corn and other grains had been milled here for years. The cottages opposite were mostly rented by miners, and a Sunday school for girls was held in one for a while, but they have now all been demolished. This area, as did the rest of the town flooded regularly – at least three or four times a year – until a flood alleviation scheme was completed in 1977. Further flood alleviation work was needed and this was completed in 2012. The mill has now been taken over for commercial use.

Woodborough Road, Radstock

It can be seen that several of the old buildings have been demolished and replaced, but many of the ranked cottages remain. The building on the left was the 'iron mission' church of St Peter and St Paul. It was built in 1890 and demolished in 1974, being replaced by a bungalow. It is a busy road that is now a large residential area with a primary school and large children's play areas, one at each end.

South Hill House, Radstock

South Hill House in about 1902; all that is left of this substantial property now are some of the original railings that surrounded the park. The house was sited at the back of its grounds and had extensive views over the countryside, including the parish church of St Nicholas nestling in the valley below. It was the home of geologist James McMurtrie, 1840–1914, the mines and estates manager for the Countess Lady Waldegrave for many years. He commenced employment in 1862: his management style led to the miners striking within months, petitioning for his removal, but he was being pushed hard to make profits by the cash-strapped countess. He had a huge influence on the area, and doubled the profits of the mines under his control. The house was demolished in the mid-twentieth century and the site was used by Radstock Technical College from the late 1940s, now Norton-Radstock College of Further Education.

Miss Rivers' Shop, Old Bath Road, Radstock

Photographed in about 1905, this tiny shop was famous with local children for its enticing selection of farthing and halfpenny sweets. Miss Rivers is on the right. Remarkably, this tiny two-up, two-down cottage supplied a huge range of everyday grocery and household goods to local people. Miss Rivers ran the shop for more than forty-five years until her death in 1949. The building was typical of the time in having no running water, electricity or gas and in sharing an outside 'privy' with several other households. It and its neighbouring buildings were demolished shortly after.

Ludlow's Pit, Radstock

Pronounced 'Ludlass' locally, and situated just off the Frome Road, this colliery was sunk in 1782 and closed in March 1954. It was a large pit, employing 375 men in June 1936. Until 1850, men descended by attaching a 'hooker' to the shaft chain, but then the shaft was opened to a diameter of 8 feet to allow men to be lowered in two cages. When the colliery closed, the red-brick pithead baths continued to be used by other local miners until their pits also closed. Today the baths and other old buildings have been converted for light industrial uses.

Writhlington School

Writhlington Secondary Modern School was not big enough for all its pupils to be taught on site until a new school was built in 1970; at the same time, it became a comprehensive school. Before this other buildings throughout Radstock were utilised for different teaching purposes. The school is now a highly regarded Business and Enterprise Academy and was completely rebuilt in 2010, winning a prestigious architectural award. Students at the school also run an internationally famous orchid propagation and conservation project.

Coombend, Radstock

The present three-storey fish and chip shop was a bicycle shop and, for a while in 1931/32, the site of the first glove factory in Radstock, Dents. Dents then moved to the premises now occupied by Swimco. To the left of the shop were the premises of Dando & Cooper, family drapers, now a private home. The present carpet warehouse premises, to the right, were built in 1816 as Radstock Methodist chapel and had been extended in 1840 to provide a schoolroom. When the chapel relocated to Fortescue Road in 1902, the property was first used as an entertainment hall and then later as the Palace Cinema, seating 450 people, before finally closing in the 1960s.

Lower Combe End, Radstock.

Coombend, Radstock

Taken in 1905, the chimney is that of the Middle Pit, which opened in 1779; by 1886 it had the deepest shaft in the Somerset coalfield. It was a large site with a wide range of buildings, including a workshop, offices and workers' cottages. During the General Strike of 1926, many policemen were billeted at the Victoria Hall, Radstock, as the pit owners expected the miners to riot. Seven months of strike, with no pay or benefits, were eventually rewarded with even less pay and more hours. It is now the site of a scrapyard, though the 1905 winding engine house and the base of the chimney still remain. Just to the south of the pit was the site of the Radstock Gas Company, which operated from the late 1850s to about 1950. The three-storey house, on the left in the picture below, was built around 1800 and is one of the oldest in Radstock.

Church of St John the Baptist, Midsomer Norton

This church is located at the west end of the town and was definitely established by 1150. The bottom of the Perpendicular tower is fifteenth century, with the top being seventeenth century. John Pinch the younger of Bath rebuilt most of the rest of the church in the Gothic style, for the Revd Augustus Asgill Colville, in 1830/31. A lady chapel was added in 1936. The interior has panelled ceilings with floral bosses and formerly had galleries. Charles II gave three of its bells; one is inscribed with 'Twas Charles the II, our gracious king, was the chief cause we eight bells ring'. Tradition says that while the King was visiting the nearby Welton Manor, he heard the peal of the cracked bells here and donated the new ones.

Church of St John the Baptist, Midsomer Norton

In 1975 lumps of decaying oak wood were found in St John's church, the remains of a rare fourteenth-century oak tomb effigy of a knight. It had certainly been on display when the Revd John Skinner of Camerton sketched it and the church in 1823, and he believed it to be of one of the Gournay family who had formerly held the Manor of Norton since the reign of Henry I. It is now thought probable that it is of one of the local Warknell family. At some point it was appropriated by local people as their 'Jack O' Lent', a surrogate Judas Iscariot, and used to be dragged through the streets at the beginning of Lent and pelted with rubbish and stones. It is now held in the Bristol City Museum for conservation, though was returned to the church for display as part of a Civic Day Service, in June 2011.

The Church of The Holy Ghost, Midsomer Norton

This building was formerly a fifteenth-century tithe barn, the tracery in the window above the porch, the style of the great doorway and the walls and buttresses being typical of that time. The owners and builders of it were the Augustinian canons of Merton Priory in Surrey, reflected in ancient recorded names for the town, 'Norton Friars' and 'Norton Canonicoram'. Following the Dissolution of the Monasteries by Henry VIII, it was given to the Crown in 1539, subsequently being in the patrimony of Christ Church, Oxford. It was later sold to a private owner in 1886, eventually being given to Downside Abbey for use as a church from 1913. It was converted by the famous architect Sir Giles Gilbert Scott, but retains many of its former features, including a rare 'granger', a small room above the porch that would have been used by the supervising monastic official when it was a tithe barn.

Church Lane, Midsomer Norton

The blacksmith's, run for many years by the Fry family, was the large building next door to the post office. They made the cemetery gates for St John's church, opposite their forge, in 1865. At a time when few people had access to a telephone, the post office would have been very busy, as sending postcards was a very popular pastime. The Hole in the Wall, in the centre distance just beyond the horse and cart, was once a brewery, and in the 1890s was lived in by William Wise the postmaster. Some cottages were pulled down in the mid-twentieth century to allow access to the Pow's Orchard car park off to the right, opposite the large building on the left.

The Priory, Midsomer Norton

This is probably the oldest surviving building in the town. It is now mostly early seventeenth century, but parts of it are thought to date back to the twelfth century. It contains many interesting features, including a restored Tudor fireplace and salt cupboard, two seventeenth-century plank doors and dado height panelling that was formerly part of the galleries in the local parish church of St John the Baptist. The land was acquired by Merton Priory, Surrey, in 1158 and then passed to Christ Church, Oxford, in about 1593. It is now The Moody Goose, a fine dining restaurant and hotel. The long building on the left, in the photograph below, is a former farmhouse that dates from the late seventeenth or early eighteenth century and was built of local limestone and sandstone rubble.

High Street, Midsomer Norton
Taken in 1906, these fine buildings have changed very little externally in the intervening years. The building in the foreground is still a bank and, at the furthest end, The Greyhound pub and restaurant was formerly a coaching inn.

High Street Towards the Square, Midsomer Norton
Casswell is still trading as a hardware store on this site and, though modernised, there are architectural features that remain identifiable. The number of horse and carts and people shows that this was a busy store.

The Old Manse, Midsomer Norton

A house and cottage existed on this site from at least 1676, though the Georgian-style frontage is probably an eighteenth-century addition. Methodist trustees bought the property in 1827 and used it as a Manse until 1897, when it reverted back to private ownership. It was demolished and replaced by a row of shops in the 1960s.

The Square, with The Island Behind, Midsomer Norton

Four Purnell brothers had stationery and printing businesses here and in Radstock and Paulton from 1839. The business developed in to a national printing and publishing concern as well as one of the largest employers in the area, until its decline and final closure in 2005. Dr Alexander Waugh, father of Arthur and grandfather of novelist Evelyn, bought the early eighteenth-century property Island House in 1865, just visible at the end of narrow road leading off the square. The Island indeed used to be an island, surrounded by the River Somer, until the river was built over to link it to the market place in the nineteenth century.

The Corn Mill, Midsomer Norton

The first documentary evidence for the corn mill dates to 1611, but there must have been one in use from at least the twelfth century. Situated on The Island, initially water from the Somer was used to power it. By 1890 the millstream had disappeared and steampower was used until the advent of electrically powered milling. The mill was still very busy in the 1950s, but eventually closed in the early 1960s, to be replaced by a small residential development.

The Fountain, Midsomer Norton

The public drinking fountain was donated by John Thatcher, the owner of the large Welton Brewery. To accommodate it in its original position, a short section of the river had to be paved over and the footpath realigned. In 1935 it was moved to a slightly different position and was then replaced by a new model in 1938, before eventually being removed altogether.

The Square, Midsomer Norton

This photograph was probably taken during the 1909 visit by the Prince and Princess of Wales. The large corner building that the five men appear to be walking towards on the right of the picture is The White Hart, a Grade II listed inn. Though there have been modernisations, many of its original features still survive. The entrance hall has a surviving jug and bottle hatch, and the bar still has the original counter and bar back, fireplace and fixed wooden benches attached to its bar walls. It was a popular meeting place for miners and other workers of the town. Slater's Directory of 1852/53 mentions it, and Kelly's Directory of 1889 records that the landlord at that time was George Talbot. The town had a thriving trade in malting and brewing in the eighteenth and nineteenth centuries.

High Street, Midsomer Norton

This photograph was probably taken on 23 June 1909, when the Prince and Princess of Wales visited Midsomer Norton to present medals to those involved in the rescue efforts following the Norton Hill colliery explosion. There is still much that is recognisable today. The Town Hall can be seen in the distance, while The Hollies is behind the wall and trees on the right. The same railings still run along the river.

Welch's Shop, Midsomer Norton

This wonderful grocer's and draper's had a 'cage' with gilded bars that the cashier would sit in. The sales assistants would put the money payments in to a wooden contraption and it whizzed through a tunnel to the cashier, who then used the same method to return the receipts. As shown below, the structure was completely rebuilt following a fire.

Silver Street, Midsomer Norton
A view towards the top of Silver Street, taken in 1912. Arthur Waugh lived in a house here from about 1868, where, in his words, 'the house was at the foot of a hill, which climbed, between an avenue, stately as a cathedral aisle, to the open fields'. His son, the novelist Evelyn Waugh, spent many childhood summer holidays in the town, staying with his maiden aunts, and later wrote, 'I suppose that in fact I seldom spent longer than two months there in any year, but the place captivated my imagination as my true home never did.'

Silver Street, Midsomer Norton

It was once a quiet, tree-lined avenue, as seen in this 1914 image. The Waugh family home was named 'Down-along', so called by the family's three unmarried sisters because the post office insisted that a name was needed for postal deliveries. The railway ran along the back of their house, crossing one of its paths, and it is said that Dr Waugh received a small sum for each train that crossed over. At one time there was a ford at the bottom of the street, a reminder of the area's propensity to flood.

Midsomer Norton Railway Station

This Somerset & Dorset Railway station opened in 1874 in Silver Street. This evocative picture shows a busy platform, as the train steams in the early 1900s. It fell victim to the Beeching cuts and closed in 1966. A group of volunteer railway enthusiasts set up the Somerset & Dorset Heritage Trust, Midsomer Norton, in 1992, in order to restore and preserve this wonderful old station and to re-lay some of its tracks.

Midsomer Norton Signal Box
This restored signal box is part of
the ongoing restoration work at
the station. There are also station
buildings, stables, rolling stock and
a buffet car, as well as a wartime
pillbox and an Anderson shelter.
The volunteers hope next to be
able to lay railway tracks as far
as the neighbouring village of
Chilcompton. The greenhouse, seen
below, was installed in line with an
original garden that was there when
the station was in use.

Town Hall and Jubilee Lamp, Midsomer Norton

The Town Hall was built by Thomas Harris Smith in 1860 in the Italianate style, on behalf of the Midsomer Norton Market Company, at a cost of £1,500. Originally, the hall had an arched and open lower concourse, but this was filled in with the walls and windows not long after. To the left of the Town Hall was the Wilts & Dorset Bank, now Lloyds. It can be seen that there was once a beautiful open space in front of these buildings. The Jubilee Lamp was donated by the Beauchamp family in 1897 and was taken down in the 1950s to improve traffic flow. The Town Hall is now used for a variety of educational and social purposes.

The 'Bath Bus', Midsomer Norton

This magnificent bus, waiting outside the side of the Town Hall in 1911, did regular runs to Bath and Bristol and had the now extinct benefit of a conductor as well as a driver. In the background, Gregory's shoe shop can be seen, now a branch of Barclay's Bank.

High Street, Midsomer Norton

Arthur Waugh wrote in 1931, 'The name of Midsomer Norton still falls upon the ear like an echo of passing music ... rural, remote, even romantic ... lanes full of flowers, and the river sparkled on its way between the cottages.' Though it is much busier, he would still recognise the High Street and many familiar buildings. The war memorial, seen below, used to stand against the wall of the building directly to the right, which had been the old brewery, then a boot factory and now shops.

Methodist Church, Midsomer Norton

In 1746, John Wesley's preachers, based in Bristol, were invited to preach in 'Midsummer Norton'. The first services were held in the cottage of a weaver named Joseph Fry and eventually a chapel was built at the junction of Rackvernal Road and Gas Lane. The local clergy and some of the local inhabitants were opposed to the building; at one point building stone was 'removed' and used to renovate the road! The chapel was eventually finished in 1775. In the early nineteenth century, a Methodist, Elijah Bush, opened a boarding school for boys in the large house in the High Street that later became a pub, now The Mallard. With further growth in numbers, the foundation stone of the present building was laid in 1858 and the church was completed the following summer. The adjoining hall was built in 1957 and both buildings have been recently renovated.

High Street, Midsomer Norton

In this image dating from the early twentieth century, on the left is the sign for the Ashton Gates off-licence and centre-right is the signpost for the Three Horseshoes pub, since demolished and replaced by a large store. Even with the renovations and new signage, the rooflines are still recognisable.

High Street, Midsomer Norton

In this image taken around 1900, on the left is Sam Lloyd's Bakery; it is still a bakery today. A little further along is Angell's, a firm of boot- and shoemakers, now with an extended frontage and trading as a toyshop. Prior to its conversion by Angell's, this had been a poorhouse, with the space divided to keep the men and the women separate. Next to Mr Angell was a barber's, then a bicycle shop, followed by the tiny 6-foot-wide Star Supply Store, formerly a lock-up, and then the River Plate butcher's, later run by the British & Argentine Meat Company. In the distance are the five almshouses, built by the wealthy Beauchamp family in 1895.

The Jersey Stores, Midsomer Norton
Also known locally as the Jersey Dairy, this property was built around 1700 and belonged to Christ Church College, Oxford. Though renovated over time, it still has original Georgian features, such as the bowed shop windows, and is still in retail use today.

High Street Floods, Midsomer Norton

Dating from the early 1970s, this is a reminder of one of the many floods that used to occur in the town. Not only the road and pavements have disappeared, but there is nothing to be seen of the River Somer that runs down the centre of the street. John Wesley visited in 1767, noting in his diary, 'Midsummer-Norton; so called I suppose, because formerly it was accessible at no other time of the year!' He was no doubt referring to the area's poor roads and tendency to flooding. To help solve the problem, a flood alleviation scheme was completed in 1977, when a tunnel to deal with excess water was laid from Somervale School in Redfield Road all the way down the High Street.

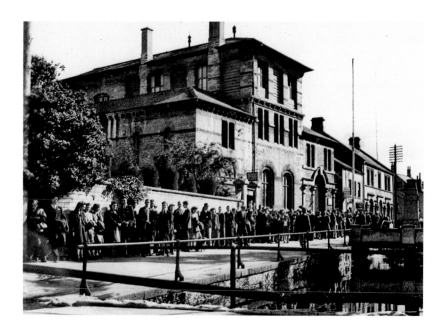

Bob's Palais de Danse, Midsomer Norton

During the 1950s, the first floor of this late eighteenth-century building was
the venue for 'Bob's Palais de Danse' and a roller skating rink. As can be seen
from the long queues, it was a very popular venue for local young people. It had
originally been part of an extensive brewery, changing and developing in usage
over the years. Where Norton Discounts is now was once Marston House, lived
in for a time by Robert Bennett, manager of Norton Hill Colliery, in the 1900s.
A small cinema named the Empire was opened just the left of the pictures in
1913. It was a tall and narrow building, with seating on just one floor. In 1934,
a balcony was added; it was completely redecorated and its name was changed
to the Palladium Cinema. It finally closed in 1993 with a showing of *Cinema
Paradiso* and is now awaiting renovation.

The Hollies, Midsomer Norton
For over 150 years this was the home of
some of the leading families of Midsomer
Norton and stood in its own extensive
parkland. Formerly known as the
Mansion House, in the 1780s the owner
had the cottage opposite demolished
and the grounds laid to lawn in order to
improve his view. Standing on the High
Street, it has been used as council offices
since 1937.

St Chad's Well and Monument, Midsomer Norton

The monument is a tall, grey stone obelisk, with plaques and carvings of regimental banners and a wreath, and stands next to the River Somer. It was erected in memory of Frederick Stukely Savage, who died in 1866, by his mother Lady Savage. It was sited in a corner of their home, Norton House, and is close to the site of a spring well. Local people used the well for their water and Lady Savage hired Mr Fry, the blacksmith, to make the railings, some of which can still be seen, in order to enclose and protect the monument. It is not clear why the spring was named after St Chad. They are now part of the site of Somervale School.

Norton House, Midsomer Norton

The Savage family built Norton House, probably on the site of an earlier manor house, and lived here during the late eighteenth and the nineteenth centuries. The family were major shareholders in the local collieries. The house was set in its own parkland and had extensive gardens, and provided employment for many local people. A Russian, Prince Tschajkowsky, lived here for a couple of years from about 1912 and spent a small fortune on refurbishing it, though he is rumoured to have eventually disappeared, leaving behind substantial debts and a reputation for being a spy! During the First World War it was used as a home for Belgian refugees. The house was demolished in about 1935 and the grounds used for residential housing and Somervale School. Volunteers have turned a small part of its former parkland in to the Silver Street Local Nature Reserve, pictured below.

Dent Allcroft Glove Factory, Midsomer Norton

In 1934 the first glove factory in Midsomer Norton was set up in a disused boot factory in Redfield Road, with part of it being used for leather treatment and finishing. The Masonic building and Shearn's garage can just be seen in the background. A path that ran down the side of the Masonic Hall was used by factory staff to reach the site and is still in use today. Weather permitting, the chamois leather sheets would be laid out on the short grass to dry. In the 1960s the factory made the leather clothing worn by Honor Blackman in *The Avengers*. The factory closed in 1972 after being gutted by fire, and the Church Court housing development for the elderly, which opened in 1978, now stands on the site.

Redfield Road, Midsomer Norton

A view of the effects of severe winter weather conditions, possibly in the 1960s, which completely froze over the River Somer. The Masonic Hall of the Connaught Lodge, with its portico and pillars, was completed in around 1912 and can be seen on the left. The garage, Midsomer Norton Motor Co., on the right of the picture, is now a petrol service station.

Stone's Cross Towards Radstock Road

The road on the left in this early twentieth-century image is Station Road, Welton, and on the right is Midsomer Norton High Street. The lamp is no more, removed to improve traffic flow with a mini-roundabout, demonstrating what a busy thoroughfare this area now is. The building on the left, with the arched window, was originally built as a Primitive Methodist schoolroom and chapel in 1907, but is now a Salvation Army citadel. The facing cottages were demolished in 1973/74.

Stone's Cross, Midsomer Norton

This view of Stone's Cross, looking towards the High Street from Station Road, probably depicts the 1911 celebrations for the Coronation of George V. Though the Welton side of the crossroads is little changed, there has been substantial rebuilding at this end of the High Street.

St Luke's Church, Midsomer Norton

Known as the 'Iron Church' or the 'Metal Mission' because of its corrugated-iron construction, this was built on Radstock Road in 1899 and acted as a mission hall and church until 1920. It was then decommissioned and used as a Church of England Men's Society venue and church hall until 1964. In that year it was bought by the Midsomer Norton Scout Group, which has used it ever since. In 1985 it was renovated and extended. Many of these mission churches were erected in North Somerset mining villages and were bought as mail order kits.

Norton Hill School, Midsomer Norton

Founded as a grammar school in 1911, Norton Hill School was built on the former site of Dimborough House, purchased for the purpose by the trustees of the Ann Harris Charity. Miss Harris, born to a wealthy Welton family, died in 1719 at twenty-two years of age and a fund was set up in her memory, initially in order to establish a charity school for forty poor children. This first school was held in a cottage in The Island from 1721. The trust also enabled the purchase of land for St John's Primary School in Redfield Road, as well as that for Norton Hill School. Sadly, The Island school cottage and Miss Harris's home in Welton were demolished in the 1960s. Though this highly-regarded school looks unchanged from this view, there are modern, purpose-built buildings behind it.

Norton Hill Colliery, Midsomer Norton

The first pit here was developed in the 1840s, but had closed by 1867. In 1896, Frank and Louis Beauchamp bought the site and sank a shaft, hiring Robert Bennett as manager. On 9 April 1908, just after 10 p.m., there was a huge underground explosion and ten miners were killed. The coal dust explosion happened about 1,500 feet underground and, as there were no official rescue teams at that time, the manager and volunteers spent ten days searching for survivors. In 1909, the Prince and Princess of Wales visited the town to award medals for bravery during and following the explosion. As a result of this and other national tragedies, the 1911 Coal Mines Act provided miners with more safety measures, including the requirement for rescue centres to be set up within 10 miles of all coal mines. The pit closed in 1966. The picture below shows part of the Old Pit Road walk and cycle track. A light industry development is on the former colliery site, at the top right in the photograph below.

Norton Hill Pit Disaster Funeral

This is the cortège of one of the 1908 funerals that followed the disaster, processing down Radstock Road and into Midsomer Norton High Street. The pit owners and manager are among the leaders of the procession. This funeral is believed to be that of William Doughty, aged twenty-one years, and Andrew Brooks, aged twenty-seven years, both of whom had lived in Radstock Road. The ten miners who had been killed ranged in age from fourteen to forty-one years.

Old Mills Pit, Paulton

Owned by the Duchy of Cornwall, this pit opened in 1860 and closed in 1966. This iconic 'batch' is notable for having been left in its original state, rather than being landscaped and planted with trees, thereby giving a good idea of the visual impact that the many slag heaps would have had in the area. A large Focus DIY store was on the site, in the foreground, for many years, but since they recently ceased trading the site is awaiting redevelopment.

The Wellsway, Westfield

Photographed in about 1908, notice the train running out of Radstock in the foreground and the fact that Somervale Road is missing. This was only constructed in 1924, having been largely funded by Sir Frank Beauchamp, a local colliery owner who paid unemployed miners to build it. The Norton-Radstock Greenway track, for walkers and cyclists, now runs along the old railway tracks. At the top right, the Wellsway Pit chimney can just be seen. This mine opened in 1829 and closed in 1920. In 1839, twelve of its miners were killed as they were being lowered underground when – it was alleged – the cage rope was cut by an unknown person and they fell to their deaths at the bottom of the shaft. The dead were aged between twelve and forty-four years; six of them were under twenty years old.

Wellsway Colliery, Westfield
Behind the young men posing playing cards, two buildings can be seen that still survive today. On the right, with the arched windows, is the old engine house, and on the left, with the low arched entrance, are the old pit pony stables. It is thought that these are the only surviving examples of such stables in the country. The chimney has long gone and the batch has been landscaped with pine trees. It is likely that the photograph to the left was taken some time after the pit closed in 1920.

St Peter's Church, Westfield

Although Westfield has only officially been a parish since the 1950s, Anglican services have been held here for much longer. Evensong was certainly being held by local miners at the beginning of the twentieth century in a house in Elm Terrace, and there have been three Anglican church buildings in Westfield since that time. The first was erected on the site of Continu-forms and then the church, pictured above, was built on the site of the present church car park in the 1950s. This was demolished in 1986 and the new church, below, was erected in 1988.

The Elm Tree Inn, Westfield

This depicts a Rogation Sunday parade in the 1950s. These parades used to be very popular and were held on the Sunday before Ascension Day, about five weeks after Easter. An ancient festival, traditionally there would be a procession around a village, with stops for hymns, prayers and readings at key points such as a farm, a river, a meadow, a garden and, in this case, a pub, finally finishing at the parish church. It was linked to blessing the crops and asking for a good harvest.

Station Road, Welton

Dating to 1931, this view is looking over the Standard Check Book Co. and the Welton Bag Co. premises. The site was formerly a large brewery belonging to the Thatcher family, which was sold to the Standard Check Book Co. in 1920. Therefore the site had long provided employment for a large number of local people. It is now the premises for the Welton, Bibby & Baron factory, still producing paper bags and packaging, though they are in the process of relocating to Wiltshire and the site's future is unclear.

The Crown Inn, Welton

It is thought that this image was taken in 1911 on the occasion of George V's Coronation. This was a very popular pub, especially as it was located almost opposite Welton train station. The building dated to the early eighteenth century, but underwent almost continuous modifications. There was an adjoining stable that latterly became used a garage. During the Second World War, American troops were billeted here and throughout Midsomer Norton, and a US Postal Service was set up in the garage. Residential homes are now located on the site.

Welton

This early twentieth-century image is taken from the Stone's Cross end of Station Road, looking towards the railway station at the top left. It is evocative of the technological changes of the period, contrasting the horse and trap on a country lane with the steam train crossing a bridge over the road in the background. The stationmaster in 1902, according to Kelly's Somerset Directory, was the wonderfully named Goldsworth Beer. The footbridge seen below, where the former railway track ran, is now part of the Norton-Radstock Greenway path.

North Somerset Brick & Tile Co., Welton

These works were in Lower Clewes and were adjacent to the station, the end of which can just be seen in the background, and made bricks and tiles for local collieries and the building industry. The works opened in 1922 and closed in 1940, with the chimney being demolished by Dawsons of Clutton in 1941. Following this, Blatchford's took over the site. Below is part of the Norton-Radstock Greenway track, part of which runs alongside the sites of the former railway station and the brickworks.

Welton Swimming Baths

Taken in 1962, this shows the only swimming pool in the area until it closed when the Wansdyke Leisure Centre opened in the 1970s. Though open-air, it was very popular with people in the surrounding area. It could be reached by three paths; one ran between the back of Clevedon Road and the Welton Rovers football ground, another between the Standard Check and the Welton Bag factories and the third ran down from Greenhill, almost opposite Monger Lane. Nothing remains of the baths, except the surprisingly small patch of ground that it occupied, now covered by trees and bushes.

Millard's Hill, Welton
Walter Harvey ran the grocery and his wife the drapery side of this shop that stood at the bottom of Millard's Hill. He is mentioned in Kelly's 1902 Somerset Directory, though not in the 1897 edition, and this image probably dates to about 1910. Harvey's shop and its adjoining houses have been demolished and replaced by a modern development, though the house just beyond remains little changed.

View Over Welton

On the left is Old Farm, dating to around the end of the seventeenth century. The cottages in the centre were demolished in 1973. The building on the right is Radstock Baptist church on West Road. Originally built for the Primitive Free Methodists in 1830, a group of Baptists, who had been meeting in a Temperance Hall in Belle Vue, bought and extended it in 1889. At the top of Millard's Hill, centre-right background, was an early isolation hospital. There was a house for the patients and the family that cared for them, Mr and Mrs Withers and their sons Pharaoh and Noah. In the 1900s, some huts were also built in the nearby field to house patients during a smallpox epidemic. The image below shows the extensive house building that has taken place in the area.

Acknowledgements

A huge debt of thanks must go to Radstock Museum, especially Nick Turner, Tom Randall, Dennis Chedgy and Martin Horler, for all their help and support. Also, much appreciation to Kim and Jeff Cottle of Midsomer Norton, Sue Lock of Writhlington School and Catriona Wooltorton of Radstock Baptist church for their help with photographs and information. My sincere thanks to David Fisher for his kind permission in allowing the reproduction of his artwork, and to Andy Pickering, of Strode College, for suggesting I do this book and for his advice. Finally, I must acknowledge with gratitude the work of Chris Howell, who published several excellent books about the area in the 1990s, an inspiration and help to me in this endeavour.

Every effort has been made to contact copyright holders; sincere apologies if I have missed anyone.

Bibliography

Dahl, Roald, *Boy: Tales of Childhood* (London: Penguin Books Ltd, London, 1984)

Horler, Moses, *The Early Recollections of Moses Horler* (Prepared and printed by Mabel Frances Coombs and Howard Coombs in Radstock, 1900)

Howell, Chris, *Some of Our Old Pictures* (Radstock: Chris Howell, 1979)

Howell, Chris, *Round Here, in Them Days* (Radstock: Chris Howell, 1980)

Jones, Reg, *Down Memory Lane, Midsomer Norton* (Radstock, 1984)

Roberts, Bettrys A., *As I Remember* (USA: Lesley J. Barker, 1991)

Vincent, Mike, *Through Countryside & Coalfield* (Yeovil, Somerset: Haynes Publications Inc., 1900)

Waugh, Arthur, *One Man's Road* (London: Chapman & Hall, Ltd., 1931)

Waugh, Evelyn, *A Little Learning: An Autobiography* (Chapman & Hall, Ltd., 1964)

Wesley, John, *The Journal of John Wesley, AM,* Vol. III (London: J. Kershaw, 1827), accessed on www.openlibrary.org

Young, Revd Ernest G. Young, *History of High Street Methodist Church Midsomer Norton 1746–1981 & of the Adjoining Hall* (Midsomer Norton: 1981)